I ROT

Copyright © 2024 by Lana Valdez

Cover by Ira Rat

This book may not be reproduced in whole or in part, except for the inclusion of brief quotations in a review, without permission in writing from the author or publisher. No part of this publication may be reproduced, stored in or introduced into retrieval system, or transmitted, in any form, or by any means (electronic, mechanical, photocopying, recording, or otherwise), without prior permission of the publisher.

Requests for permission should be directed to filthylootpress@gmail.com

"You know how the first time you got invited over to a hot girl's apartment you realized that with the exception of the carefully curated corner of the living room that has good lighting where she takes all her selfies there's just mountains of stained clothes and rotten DoorDash and the whole place smells like litter box? I Rot feels like that realization in book form."

- Jonathan Blake Fostar (Editor in Chief, Dream Boy Book Club)

"A haunting experimental narrative that puts religious fervor in a new light. I read this in one sitting and couldn't bring myself to put it down, and I felt like I was rubbernecking at a highway car accident. Small towns, drunk nuns, and commandments that all come together in a chilling finale. When it comes to Lana's work, the devil really is in the details."

- Paula Macena, (author of *Penance of the Byronic Hero*)

"With each verse, Lana's breath forms a deliciously macabre and visceral new realm I have yet to discover. These Plath-like fables are reminiscent of a place where dreams and nightmares converge, and like a shovel they begin to unearth the inevitable dirt you have on your own psyche."

- Mariya Stehnitska

I ROT
LANA VALDEZ

filthyloot.com

THE RED DOLL

The Flower King

Florida was the land of
callery pear trees, of growing up black and blue,
learning what
hands and mouths could do

I dragged my tongue across all his
shaky blue veins
When we're bad, we're better

Licking fingers stained
pink by entrails,
a fuzzy nose enclosed in your palm.
The nicest boy in the whole town

Only you could make
butterflies out of bruises, you
The angel boy
with the weird face

Days in teacups,
days spinning in poppy fields until the
desert runs out of air and
we can't see our hands, we
the sons of the prickly trees

Eloise

My parents will let me walk wherever, so it's really
up to you where we go.
Are you worried about seeing the room,
is that the thing you say
haunts your nights?
I stopped dreaming nightmares and tales years back,
and my breath got chilly,
not like a mint but a sharp snowbird,
is that how you felt?
Did you feel your heart clutch in your cold hands?
There's no need to wander back to my street,
there are no bad dreams
chasing us tonight.

The Red Doll

I was maybe hellbent on tearing up everything under
our roof and the church
without stopping for a spritz of holy water or a
maple donut from next door. Dark matter
falls from the sky, it's my thirteenth May

but it was before I touched the red doll, so I still
gnawed off skin in fear of earth eaters, I knew
nothing I could've lied until all my teeth fell out

Outside in the parking lot, someone left their hair-
it's attached to a hat, with tire marks all over it,
roadkill
I would've watched while I drank my strawberry
milk, and cheered on
its demolition but I was accidentally seven Mays too
late

I might've been locked in the church basement for a
while now, because a
new child and his jelly donut have taken my spot
my spot from four Mays ago

when I thought I was a haunted girl
If a monster wasn't enough for me to leave, I don't know what would be-
maybe all the entrails they never even cleaned up, or all the tire marks in the parking lot,
one for every
May I was gone but never really gone, one for all the different women
and their frozen expressions I've seen
in the mirror behind me
since I touched the red doll

Diary Entry #1

Lately I fear I'm inviting ghosts in my prayers. I think,
is it normal to fear my prayers?

Is it safe in this house?

Stewart

In the mornings I studied the paintings of the women, their butts toned and golden, long braids down their back and baskets of fruit, bread rolls.

The antiseptic white couch, scrubbed clean of sticky fingers, a touch of banality. But the Kristy Kreme boxes on the counter were from days before, maybe even weeks, and the poinsettias were beginning to rot.

My grandmother kept vases of poinsettias everywhere, even in the summer. Every corner left a scar, all the times I'd come down, sweating, watching the dog run from my lap down to the lake, again and again. All the times my mother told me she loved me to get me away.

I wondered how bad it really was, how quickly my infectiousness spread.

Languid, like Snails

My mother stands in the kitchen,
swatting flies, plants vying with open mouths
overfed.
They are not the only ones
My brother and I,
plump yarn dolls stuck together with rug burn,
stretch marks, odd bones,
stuck together at the trestle table
and she waits for us.

Little Lords of the Sea

In a playground in a village by the sea,
something cracks. It's not the ruins
of muddy plaid skirts,
or the seashells that found their way
from the main beach,
but this little mania.
A leader, who is fearless and fly-esque,
leads them all through the darkness-
and they've been waiting for this
for a long, long time.

Ash Wednesday

In Friday Mass, I fold my skin from the inside out,
inhale
the sweetness of black dust from my fingertips.
I will return there one day,
will hang upside down in the violent sky

Watch the priest, his nose cracked and bloody,
the boys who will do whatever he says.
My nails dig into my brain, and the girls
are watching me now, narrowing their eyes,
whispering, *Why is she so smart?*
Does she know who we go home to
when we die?

Diary Entry #2

Dear diary,
I have passed on the opportunity to meet God.
When I had the chance to meet him,
or meet whoever my classmates spoke in whispers to,

I was busy worshiping something else
I was chasing after.

Now I think I feel my soul starting to decay,
just like they said it would.

Strange Lakes

Out of the seven or eight bedrooms I have lived in, I can only remember Rainberry Lake, the room I was afraid to sleep in, the room I watched the dust particles float by in bed and first noticed I had dandruff. It had high ceilings, windows that scratched against the cypress trees at night, sprinkling evil over my head while I slept. My grandma tried to drive them all out when she visited, refusing to sleep in my bed but praying the Rosary in it, again and again, the too big room. Too big for a child, too close to the edge of the lake.

Once, four of us found a coral snake curled at the foot of the bed, the same sleepover where we prank called people for the first time and Mary called her parents at two in the morning just to tell them she loved them. Years later, we found out they had been forcing her to drink bleach when she didn't finish her homework on time. I wanted something to color my life, to darken it.

I dreamed that one of us would walk down to the dock and not come back when morning came, to be declared missing for years until the day a small, mummified twelve year old body was pulled out of the Intercoastal- bits of shoulders, and toes missing, gone with the hammerhead sharks.

Boy

Through his eyes, trekking along the beaten path
he stops to watch
girls like ice cream sundaes.

Trunk or Treat

My first day at St. Paul's landed on Halloween, and I stuck out as a gawky, tall kid that came at a weird time, since my mom had to pull strings to get me accepted. She bought me a cheap witch costume from Savers and painted my nails dark purple, almost black, and I wondered what they would think of this. In the news that week, a fifteen year old boy shot up an elementary school and gutted eleven kids, and one teacher. I was nine.

The first day went blurringly well; I said my name when prompted by the nuns, smiled at three girls and one smiled back, a chunky Italian girl with glasses, and we ate cold pizza in the classroom for lunch, since it had started to rain. Out the window, huge puddles lay seeping into the concrete and on the playground, the mulch looked wet. I wondered what would happen if I ventured onto the swing set anyways, if I would slide clean off. The Italian girl, Isabella, asked me if I was going to Trunk or Treat, the school's Halloween event where we trick-or-treated in the parking lot and parents had to decorate their cars. "Um, I don't think my parents want to decorate their car," I said slowly, and Isabella nodded, she understood. She wasn't allowed to celebrate Halloween, her family was very religious. Before I knew it, the day was over and I waited next to Isabella at pickup, where all the kids were gathered. My mom smiled when she pulled up and saw me, probably happy that I made a friend that looked like a nice girl, not a boy. In the car, she didn't take her sunglasses off. "Jesus, it's like Lord of the Flies out here," she said, driving away.

Rain was still on the ground and the sky had turned dark purple by the time we parked our car in the lot, shining with orange lights and mini pumpkins my mom and I had found at the grocery store. My parents didn't dress up, but my mom at least pulled on a pair of devil ears, and I wondered if the nuns would be there, if they would say anything. The two of them laughed a lot, passing a clear bottle back and forth between them. When my mom caught me staring she hissed, in kind of a funny way, "Look around, everyone's getting hammered."

When I looked around, I didn't see any small clear

bottles, but I saw foldout tables covered in pizza boxes, platters of wings, big bottles of wine and packs of beer hidden underneath tables. I understood this was a party for adults, not for kids to go trick-or-treating. I looked around for Isabella, wishing she was allowed to come. A nice, plain-looking couple approached my parents, smiling, holding up the bottles of wine. The woman wore scrubs, and my mom acted like she knew her. Maybe she did. I wondered if my parents would drink as much as they did at home, and I decided to go look for other kids in my class.

A girl named Lucia found me first, she had really curly hair. She seemed like one of the popular girls, but she was being nice to me so I didn't question it. She grabbed my hand, and we started running towards the playground, where she said the other kids were. A song about kids running faster than someone's gun played faintly in the background. I heard it on the radio a lot at that time.

We all stood together on the playground, a jumbled mess of kids in costumes- me in my witch costume, Lucia as Alice in Wonderland, boys dressed as soldiers or mini monsters. A boy with dark eyes and freckles called for our attention, and he held up a flashlight to show his face clearer. "Since it's Halloween, we're going to play Bloody Mary. Let's go to the bathrooms by the cafeteria," and we went running again. I felt a strike of panic go through me, and I clutched Lucia's hand tighter. She didn't seem scared.

In front of the cafeteria, the boy who was the leader was having trouble opening the doors. The school building was probably locked, since it was after hours. He kicked the door, angry. We wondered how we would get the doors to open, all riled up and knowing that it was extremely important for us to do something like this. I didn't know why, but I felt it too.

Suddenly, a younger boy with really tan skin and big brown eyes brought the flashlight to his face. He looked pleading. "You guys, we can't do this," he said. "'Thou shalt have no false gods before me.' It says that in the ten commandments. We can't talk to Bloody Mary."

A silence fell over all of us, realizing his words. I hadn't thought about the fact that I was breaking a commandment, and I wondered if it was even a mortal sin. I shivered. The boy who was the leader nodded, and put his hand on the younger boy's shoulder. "Okay,

Ben is right. Let's play tag!" and we ran towards the playground one more time. A pack of us, like small, clumsy wolves.

I couldn't run as fast as the other kids, my legs were too long and I never learned how to properly use them, so I struck out first and watched the rest of the group run around in circles, ducking under slides and hiding behind fat tree trunks. It was so dark I couldn't see their faces, could only make out the shadows of their bodies. I wondered if my parents were okay back there, and figured that if they were the most drunk, that other people like that couple would take care of them. I decided I liked my new school, and thought it was cool that kids actually tried to follow the ten commandments.

I heard a weird sound, and turned my head to see what was happening. The kids were all gathered around the monstrous tree trunk, the tops of their heads cut off by darkness. They were all looking at something, and I wondered if someone fell and got hurt. Lucia called me over.

When I got closer, I saw that it wasn't a kid that fell and got hurt but someone big, and tall. One of the parents. A man lay on the ground, moaning. At first I thought he was just tired. But I saw hot and red liquid pouring out of the side of his head, where it looked like the skin folded over itself. To my horror, I saw that he was holding a clear bottle in his hand, just like the one my parents drank from outside of the car.

"Who is that?"

"Isn't that Isabella's dad?"

"Should we go tell our parents?"

"He's drunk," I said, my voice sounding weird and far away, like it wasn't my voice. All the kids turned and looked at me. It was the first words I had spoken all night, besides to my parents.

"How do you know?"

"I've never seen a drunk person before."

"Neither have I."

The boy who was the leader took a step closer to the man on the ground, who sounded like he was having trouble breathing. It always bothered me that I never learned the boy's name, and all these years later, only remember him by this one night, nothing more. He looked frozen, like he didn't know what to do.

Then, Ben's voice. "Drunkards will not inherit the

kingdom of God."

    Another solemn silence fell over us, and I heard the song again in my head: about running, running, running from a gun. We became little soldiers of God, would go on to become beautiful husbands and wives united under God when we were older, but that night were just soldiers, like good children are meant to be. It didn't even feel weird, all the red and pink stuff a mess on the concrete, and how my shins hurt the next day from all the kicking. We wanted to make God proud.

SEDUCTION

Dreams in Aramaic

In the morning,
we drink the pages of Ezekiel like coffee.
You say it is scratched onto my heart,
brutal love in scrawl.

I don't know when we became this way,
naming countries in our sleep

Getting so scared we wake with
teeth sticking like glue
whispering our names until we forget them,
snakes with cold hands

Saffron

You were the one who was doing it.
I never caught you,
only caught myself
sniffing the air around me

when dead ants
on the counter became
sage spiced
and dead hair became
saffron.

I never caught you, but in my dreams
you were doing it-

bathing in strange water,
tucking stones
in my pockets
while the lamb smoked
and smoked.

I sleep in your bed,
and I feel your hands on me
when I'm alone.

Real Love

I can sit, and you can teach me about the real world
until my brain hurts.
The baby doe watches me from the corner-
she's growing too big for your closet.

Shutters

In the eye of the real hurricane,
there are no shutters. Only you and me,
holding down the stars.

In the junk shop,
I find the Mayan calendar-
wheels of thread spinning through gold pages,
ancient tongues,
eyeballs wrapped in silk.

There are no seers anymore, you say.

The Other Angel

The fever is sweet today, peach pie air and angels in their straight lines,
their plump-faced babies and their babies and their butter-ball cheeks.

If I close my eyes, I can feel it-
his pupils and my pupils almost touching, how they swell with a look
and a brush of the right fingers, too-big balloons of flesh and shame.

I smile at other boys, I bare my teeth,
but the other angel lurks in the air, his nose on my nose,
his fever settling under my skin.

Diary Entry #3

as the others taste and see,
I just watch
maybe I'm from a better place-
some untouched, godless
planet

My Prettiest Summer

You are a much more serious thing than i ever
thought you could be,
you are a man.
And even though I dreamt you up from nothing but
blacktop dust and obsidian,
I am no more scared of you than I should be

or the way you stare at me
through the cabin window–
you've scared the other campers,
their dreamcatchers sway
and take flight in the flames
and they drop,
drop,
drop like flies

A Lover's Quarrel

I keep thinking about when you went hungry
for too long
and you bit into me,
blackberries bursting from my cartilage,
shivers on your flesh as the poison filled my cheek

We keep coming back to these roles,
me on the operating table and

you on the prowl.

Goodbye, diary.

sometimes I think I still love you,
though now I know you could never love me back.

I cry for you every day,
like my body is wondering if I made right choice
choosing you over God.

Gold Star Manners

Your father taught you gold star manners,
reading fortunes and palms
behind closed doors and
opening them for me, the parasite
And the gifts he gave you earned you
a seat at the shelter
when the skies turn yellow
and the clouds turn to ellipses
Maybe I will find the house off the beaten path,
fire in my hair

A Real Writer's Retreat

She called it a real writer's retreat weekend, and whisked us both away as soon as church was over and my mom was already on her way back home. She wouldn't have approved of our whispering and planning while the priest laid out his beautiful cloth and sang his hymns, we were in the house of God, and in His house, there are no other plans.

In the car, she played the same Blood Orange song for a while until she grew tired of it, and then the rain stopped on the freeway and projected a huge rainbow onto the sky. It wasn't really rainbow weather. We got to the motel just around the time her face started to twitch a bit, something that usually happened when unexpected weather occurred. I liked the motel, it was ratty and seemed like it was housing very interesting people, like the crack addicts I had seen in the documentary about our town's drug problem. The motel might have been the hotspot of the short little movie; I remembered the name as being Seashell Palace something or other. Once, as a little girl, I had gotten head lice from an infested bed at the Shell Cottage, the same place where my mom bought me a shirt that said "Princess of Broward County."

    She had said we were going only to write, that we couldn't continue depriving ourselves any longer of our bursting creative minds and souls. Every day, I felt like I was closer to imploding, when I couldn't open my mouth and say the weird shit I wanted to and couldn't record every single thought onto paper. She had packed a bag with some moisturizing sheet masks, two notebooks, a pack of number two pencils, unsharpened, a little baggie of shrooms, some gas station peanut butter crackers, and little bottles of Tito's vodka, that clinked around in her purse while she talked to the front desk lady, which made me self conscious. I wished I was like her, and suffered no consciousness, had no care in the world to become socially inept. We spent about an hour and a half putting on our face masks and sitting around on the beds, and she talked about how she was going to be starting her next story. It was about a mother who prayed for the deaths of her children, two sons and a daughter, because she felt they robbed her of her life. When the day came the children all died in a shooting, she told me, she wept out of complete sadness and regret, and vowed to never allow herself to feel happiness or love ever again as punishment. I said nothing, just listened.

We did a good job relaxing, something that she said was extremely essential to our writing process. She was my idol, I had never known any other artists in my life. I put on the cucumber eye patches and let it sting the insides of my eyes, watching them grow redder, like they were blushing. The TV looped infomercials about drugs for arthritis and heart problems in the background, but we were listening to music. She sang songs she liked, I would write poems inspired by them later. She started drinking. It was nearly midnight, and all my notebook pages were blank. She suggested we take the lawn chairs from our patio area and drag them over to the front door of our room, so we could really breathe in the night air as we soaked up our inspiration. We were so far from the ocean.

My notebook was laid in my lap, sideways so I could write how I liked, up and down instead of sideways, something I always thought was weird. I didn't hear cicadas, my senses were expanded enough to capture other noises. I looked over at her and she was staring out into the blackness, clenching one of the bottles in her fist. I closed my eyes, I knew what was coming. She would drink and talk, drink and talk, just so I could absorb it all up. She was not self serving in the least, she offered up her troubles and pains for me on a silver platter so I could use everything. I gulped it up. I started drinking, too, the misty humid air pulling me into a delightful chokehold, where I happily strayed from breathing. Dragonflies buzzed and hopped around us. The clinking of the bottles melted into something pleasant, something I would never be embarrassed of. It became the sound of love, between her and I, the person who loved me the most. My pages were filled with her, I felt like exploding. My throat and eyes were scorching hot and burning me, like they were eggs being fried on the sidewalk on TV. Hot, puffy tears dripped down my face when I tried to open them. She had done this to me, the best thing that another person could have done for me. I would give up absolutely everything for this feeling, of being

the greatest writer on Earth.

RAPTURE

Him and I

I give you my hands, but you wanted blood.
Yours, chilled to the bone and emptied, make repairs
to the stained cherry oak, the wooden table
that is already outliving us.

It's cold in the living room and we are sick,
in God's house where the roof is starting to crumble.
I knew you

long before we burned them all down, drank up
their mother tongues and whispered their names in
our sleep,

before the rivers ran red and
we descended on the world,
tongues and fire.

Safe

I want to tell her
that she'll be far away before the sky pours fire
and ash onto our heads,
that the highway will one day crumble and
make a bone graveyard out of our taxi drivers
but she is already gone

Ripe

The sky is sunless, like it should be.
Last night,
I sat in a circle of people I didn't know
and denounced my father

We emptied the river basins of their anchors,
threw them
yonder scaffold high
until his skin became stone
his tongue curled back.

Last night I drank pumpkin rot,
from the ground to my lips.
In the dream,
they looked at me
and knew I was looking at them

Maybe they died of fear,
while I slept so
soundlessly.

I think
I might still have dirt
under my tongue.

A-minor Sonata KV-130

I tell my girls about Amadeus,
how his grand keys
whirled into blue silk scarves in the sky,
how they would fall around the
slender shoulders of the women and into their
mouths.

How he could turn the beaten pulp of ugly
into pinked cheeks.
I tell them how their beauty isn't scary, how
if they wanted to, they could
burn the curl-de-sac clean,
white light.

I remember when my life revolved around
the songs I sang at night. I remember when my life
revolved around
the boys who tore me open with glass.

I remember these things and
hold my girls close at night,
when the bugs creep into the master bedroom,

and their faces light up in their sleep.

Hypochondriac

Get dressed, it's time for the body report!
There's not a healthy bone in your corse, or any
magic in your ailing blood.
A lick of your neck will tell me all I need to know,
you can lie back now.

In your cave, you spin out and
spin out until your brains are oozing from the floor,
the walls

Your skin is dry from the inside out,
and you can hear the elders pulling you away,
whistling through their sweetly rotting teeth, rising
carcasses

In heaven, this child will be well.

The Farmhouse Gang

Downstairs at the table,
the fish have disappeared,
exoskeletons on pearl plates.
The incense has ruined us

we weave tales of
farms on lakes of ice,
Norsemen with flesh in their teeth

The talking has ruined us,
catfish and hollow eyed children
on our knees.

Many in the Mirror

My fingers, cold and dipped in charcoal
stain my face, the corners of my mouth
ripe at the sides.

I'm looking in the mirror and there's fingers all over
my face-
they're all wrong, fistfuls of mulch and leaves
from the fallen treehouse

I'm looking for my father in the mirror, and there's
fingers pressed to my temples,
reverberating with sound

Praying

When I know it's time to go, I'll start to bruise from
the inside out-
from the weak rib where he made me,
to the hair I grew down my back.
You'll take a picture of me at my most beautiful,
right before the worms find their way in,
and make sure my brain is insured, not my body.
Nothing else matters now,
not how they used to call me a strange beauty,
or how my roots will darken
into the earth, deeper, deeper, deeper.

Happy, Holy Day

On the morning of the wedding, I find two deep, identical cuts on the backs of my ankles, as if I've been slashed in my sleep. When I bend down to look, I can see bits of bone. I show this to Marla, worried she is going to judge my body for not being perfect on this holy day, but she is nonchalant about my physical appearance, telling me that there are far more important things at play today. "Remember," she says, "you are a holy vessel."

I try not to think about the cuts and dress myself silently out in the garden, so I don't have to be oohed and awed at in the communal bathroom, and decreasing the chances I run into Julian before the ceremony. The dress isn't mine, it was gifted to me by Marla and the other girls, obviously very old and ripping open in one of the armpits. Luckily, it happens to look beautiful on me, and I stand and admire myself in the one mirror we keep in the backyard. I tell myself it's in happiness, not in vain.

Soon, the girls all flit out of the house, giggling and bumping into each other like nervous butterflies. They take me by the hand and lead me out to the fields we have on the property, long sprawling hills of meadows that we can run and dance and jump in, and I am reminded of my first day on the property: holding Francesca as she cried, loudly, that she needed to come back here, needed to see Horace and Marla and everyone, and walking her back from the car, then becoming surrounded by everyone. I thought for a second that I should have been scared, but they were all so beautiful and interesting: a side of California I had not seen in the years I had moved from Broward County, from the dusty souvenir shops and wet marshes. All of them had tan, freckled skin, from spending hours lounging and laying in the sun, playing music. At dusk, we all gathered around a wooden table for dinner and I let Horace and Marla take my hands and learn about my ghosts, all of them, the newer ones and the ones from when I was a little girl: the doll, the man by the tree trunk, the possessed boy.

It had been a long time since I met other people who had seen ghosts like these before, or had any themselves. Before, it was only Francesca, but at that point she was beginning to slip. Still, once I was asked to live in the compound, I curled up next to her on the bottom bunk and held her while she cried. Her ghosts had started to come back.

For a long time, I stayed on the compound and helped the women with our special duties: assisting with dinner, chopping wood for the fire, Marla even taught me how to sew so I could make dresses for the little girls. But I didn't know what my purpose was, how I was supposed to help the family. They had their own customs and rules, traditions that were made before I joined and didn't know the origins of. They told me it was good for me to stay uneducated about some things, and I believed that it was for the greater good, to just obey. It wasn't until Julian joined that my purpose was revealed to me, and by then it was too late for me to change anything. And I truly didn't know if they knew.

Every time I looked at him, I knew he knew. He remembered every single detail, how he slipped me sharpened pencils and gum in the classroom but tripped me roughly on the playground, until I skinned both of my knees, in the same spot. Stigmata, he later revealed to me as he slipped onto the log I was sitting on by the fire. He had wanted to give me the same cuts, like he was playing God. When I look at him,

I see his eight year old face: pinched and sharp, every part of his face angry, like he was angry at me for being alive. I think of breathing in dirt, his shoe resting on the top of my head and coughing up mulch for days. He had always to get close to me, he murmured in my ear that same night.

So once I agreed, wedding arrangements were to be made immediately. Marla and Maddie and all the women found a dress for me to wear, probably from Horace's mother's special trunk, where even Marla was not allowed to look in. The women gathered things for the wedding dinner, and I was prepared the way an animal gets ready for the slaughter. I was fed the best meals cooked by Marla, before even the men got to eat, I got to sit in the garden and read books about marriage that Marla gave to me, about heaven and unity. I chose to believe that they didn't know, they would never place me in harm's way. I ate all my meals, posed for measurements in case the women had to alter my dress, I paid closer attention to the children in case it was required of me to produce a child. I did not see Julian for weeks, a tradition that he not be allowed to see the bride. I wondered, if when we were standing together in unity, I would find him handsome.

It is now nearing twelve o'clock and the ceremony is about to start. I am in my dress, and did my hair the way they told me, and the girls surround me. We danced for nearly an hour, and I almost felt happy at the day, how sunny it was, how pleased Horace and Marla look as I stand in front of them. Vessel of God.

Julian steps out of the house, crisp and in white. When he steps forward to take my hands, I'm seized with fear. Horace and Marla don't seem to notice, and continue tying my hands together behind my back, in symbolization of how I'm going to serve Julian as a wife, and by doing so serve God. A warmth shoots up from my stomach to my throat, and feels dangerous. I wonder if I might drop dead of a heart attack, and if I would still go to heaven. Incapacitated and unable to move my hands, I now look Julian fully in the eyes, dark orbs floating around the sharp corners of his face. They detect nothing, but he smiles at me.

I wear a veil made of crushed flowers made by the little girls, who hope to grow up and give themselves the same way I am doing now. I think Julian is a miracle, the way he is able to make butterflies from bruises, the way his father taught him and his grandfather before, and I realize everyone knows. Everyone knows what he did to me, they can see through his pink cheeked little boy face, and they know what he did to me, and what will happen.

TALENTED PERVERTS™

Talented Perverts is a wholly owned subsidiary of Filthy Loot Enterprises.

Shane Jesse Christmass - Meth-dtf
Alex Osman - Scandals
Charlene Elsby - Letters to Jenny Just After She Died
Ira Rat - The Medication
Ira Rat - Endless Now
Various - Little Birds (series)

PERPETUAL NOSTALGIA FOREVER®

www.ingramcontent.com/pod-product-compliance
Lightning Source LLC
LaVergne TN
LVHW092059060526
838201LV00047B/1462